A First Look at Art

Families

Ruth Thomson

Chrysalis Children's Books

First published in the UK in 2003 by
Chrysalis Children's Books
An imprint of Chrysalis Books Group Plc
The Chrysalis Building
Bramley Road, London W10 6SP

ISBN 1 84138 706 1

British Library Cataloguing in Publication Data
for this book is available from the British Library.

Editorial manager: Joyce Bentley
Editor: Susie Brooks
Designers: Rachel Hamdi, Holly Mann
Picture researchers: ilumi, Aline Morley
Illustrator: Linda Francis
Photographer: Steve Shott
Consultant: Erika Langmuir, formerly Head
of Education, The National Gallery, London

The author and publishers would like to thank
Hazel Mills and pupils at Lady Bay Primary
School, West Bridgford, and Elizabeth Emerson,
for their contributions to this book.

Printed in China

Picture acknowledgements

Front Cover: Scala, Florence, The Art Institute
of Chicago 1990
4: National Gallery, London; 5: Collection of Mississippi
Musuem of Art ; 6/7: Courtesy of the Woolgar Family,
Firle Place, Sussex; 10/11: Scala, London/MOMA/© Kahlo
Estate; 11: © Kahlo Estate; 14: Courtesy of the Robert. B.
Mayer Family Collection/©Escobar Marisol/VAGA, New
York/DACS, London 2003; 15: Reproduced by permission
of the Henry Moore Foundation; 18/19: ©Photo RMN/
Gérard Blot; 22: Scala, Florence, The Art Institute of
Chicago 1990; 23: National Portrait Gallery, London;
27: Bridgeman Art Library/©DVID Hockney.

Contents

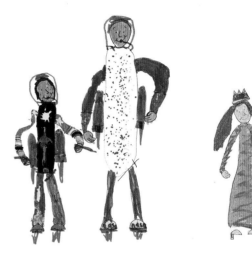

FAMILIES FOREVER

Throughout history, artists have portrayed all kinds of families – large and small, rich and poor, happy and sad, old and young. In this book you'll see a selection of family portraits. You will find out what inspired the artists and learn about their techniques. There are also questions to help you look at the works in detail, and ideas for creating your own family pictures and sculptures.

◉ You'll find answers to the questions and information about the artists on pages 30-31.

Arty tips

✦ Look out for Arty tips boxes that suggest handy techniques and materials to use in your own work.

Picture hunt

✦ Picture hunt boxes suggest other artists and artworks that you might like to look at.

The Graham Children
William Hogarth
1742
(160.5 x 181cm)

Family meanings

Artists portray families for different reasons. Hogarth painted the children on the left for their wealthy parents. The baby died while the picture was being made, so Hogarth included symbols, such as cut flowers and fruit, as reminders of the shortness of life.

Lawrence's painting, on the right, is not a portrait of one particular family. It represents the artist's belief that all people should live in harmony. Lawrence shows people of different races working together. The happy family link hands and all walk with the same foot forward.

Spotting clues

When you look at family portraits, think about what they mean. Study the pose of each figure. Does one person stand out more than the rest? If so, why? What does the setting say about the family's lifestyle?

Reading relationships

See what you can tell about the family relationships. Do people touch one another? Do they turn their heads towards or away from one another? Do the shapes and colours of their clothes match or contrast?

The Builders
Jacob Lawrence
1974
(76.2 x 56.2cm)

5

John, Count of Nassau-Siegen, and his Family

Anthony Van Dyck

1634 (292.5 x 265cm)

Before photography was invented, wealthy people asked well-known artists to paint their family portraits. These hung on display in their grand houses. Artists made sure they presented the family as impressively as possible, showing off their great wealth and status.

◉ Search for some clues that show this family's importance:

- their coat of arms
- the carved names of each person

- expensive clothes made of silk, satin, lace and velvet
- luxurious textiles – tapestries, curtains and rugs
- fine jewellery

Family relationships

Family portraits often looked to the future. They emphasised the importance of the first-born son, who would take on the family title and property. Notice how the pose and placing of these parents and children give clues about their relationships. The important-looking man and his wife are joined on a raised platform by their son and heir.

◉ How does the father indicate that the son is his heir?

◉ What can you guess about the boy's character from the way he is standing?

◉ Which is the eldest daughter? What clues tell you this?

FAMILY MATTERS

Our place

What is the place like where you and your family belong? How would you show it in a picture?

◉ Draw portraits of people in your family. Glue them down one side of a large sheet of coloured card.

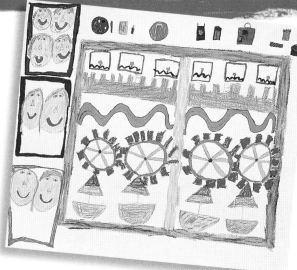

Cassie, aged 8

◉ On another piece of card, draw several images that represent your particular place. Choose things that are important to you.

◉ Glue this picture next to your family portraits.

Maisie, aged 8

Adam, aged 9

Arty tip

✿ Why not repeat your favourite or most important images to form a pattern? Use a tracing or a template, or cut a simple shape from a potato and use it to print.

Surprising snaps

Take some snaps of your family around your home or out and about. When you look at them, you may be suprised to see what they show about relationships in your family.

Joanna, aged 8

Daisy, aged 13

Family coat of arms

Make a family coat of arms, with clues about the activities and hobbies of people in your family.

◉ On stiff card, draw a crest shape (see examples below). Cut it out.

◉ Divide the crest into four panels by drawing coloured lines.

◉ Think of a picture clue for each person and draw it in one of the panels. If there are more than four people in your family, put more than one clue in each panel. If there are fewer, you could include pets, cousins or even friends.

Examples of picture clues might be:

dog or cat........ pawprint or bowl
travel................. car, train or aeroplane
gardening......... flower or watering can
cooking............. saucepan or spoon
baby.................. bottle, rattle or teddy

What others can you think of?

Becky, aged 7

Ayaz, aged 7, and Duncan, aged 9

Mollie, aged 8

Picture hunt

☆ Look for crests in pictures of grand and royal families. The colours and symbols each have a meaning – a bear symbolises strength, a lion is a sign of bravery and fur is a mark of dignity. Red is the colour of a warrior, purple is royal and blue symbolises loyalty.

A FAMILY TREE

My Grandparents, My Parents and I (Family Tree)
Frida Kahlo
1936 (30.79 x 34.73cm)

A family tree is a way to show how family members of different generations are linked. Here, Frida Kahlo tells us how she is related to her parents and her two sets of grandparents.

◉ What has Frida used to link the people in her family tree? Why do you think it is red?

Frida and her home

Frida has painted herself as a two-year old, standing in the patio of the house where she was born. It was built by her father in the suburbs of Mexico City.

Frida's parents

The portraits of Frida's parents are based on their wedding photograph (*right*). The fuzzy cloud effect in the two floating portraits of her grandparents was inspired by this photo, too.

◉ What differences can you see between the photograph of Frida's parents and their painted portraits?

Frida's grandparents

Frida's mother had Mexican parents, but her father's family came from Germany. Notice how Frida suggests where her grandparents came from. Her Mexican grandparents hover over the rugged, dry land of Mexico, whereas her German relatives float above the ocean.

◉ Who is the strongest character in the painting? How do you think Frida felt about this person?

Wedding Photograph of Frida Kahlo's Parents 1898

FAMILY TIES

Draw your own family tree

Draw a family tree that shows the links between you and several generations of your family.

Billie, aged 8

Lily, aged 7

your mother or step-mother's parents

your father or step-father's parents

your mother and father or step-mother or step-father

you and your sister(s) or brother(s)

Becky, aged 7

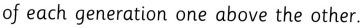

◉ Starting with yourself, draw pictures of your family, with people of each generation one above the other.

◉ Link the people together with lines to show how they are are connected.

A photographic family tree

If you have old photographs of your relatives, make a photo family tree.

◉ Ask someone to take photos of you, matching the poses of the old photos.

◉ Scan or take photocopies of the old photos. Use them side by side with your photos to make a decorated family tree.

Picture hunt

✰ Look at pictures that show other ways of depicting several generations, such as **She ain't Holding them up: She's Holding on: Some English Rose!** by Sonia Boyce, and **Many Happy Returns of the Day** by William Powell Frith.

Indi, aged 11

A family tree collage

Make a collage tree decorated with pictures of your family.

◉ Paint or stick separate portraits of people in your family on plain fabric.

◉ Glue ribbon or lace around each picture to make a fancy frame.

Sadie, aged 10

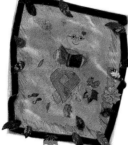

Jiang Jiang, aged 10

Jessica, aged 10

Eden, aged 11

Frances, aged 11

Sadie, Jiang Jiang, Holly, Naomi and Jessica, aged 10, and Frances and Eden, aged 11

◉ Cut out a tree trunk from brown fabric.
◉ Stick on fabric branches and leaves.
◉ Glue your pictures on to the tree, with you at the bottom, your parents above, your grandparents above them and so on.
◉ Link the generations with coloured cord, ric-rac, wool or ribbon.

Arty tips

✪ You could glue on embroidery thread, wool or cotton wool for hair and beards.

✪ Decorate the frames with sequins and cut-out flowers. Try to create an old-fashioned look for the older generations.

MODEL FAMILIES

These two sculptures of families are larger than life. Neither portrays a particular family. Instead, both express an *idea* about families.

◉ What immediate differences can you *see* between these two families? Compare the poses and the arrangements of the figures. Compare the different materials.

The Family
Marisol
1963
(201cm high)

All dressed up

Marisol's sculpture (*left*) pokes fun at a family who have dressed up smartly to go for a stroll. Perhaps they mean to be serious, but Marisol makes this a joke.

◉ How does Marisol show the serious nature of the family?

◉ What differences are there in the way Marisol's mother and father are sculpted?

◉ What's odd about the girl with the doll and the feet in the pram?

Mixed media

Marisol mixed ready-made objects with painted blocks of wood and wood carving.

◉ Which are ready-made objects? What has been carved or painted on wood?

Family togetherness

Henry Moore sculpted this family group soon after he became a father himself. It reflects his own idea of being part of a family.

Moore first made a small model of the sculpture out of plaster. Then he had it enlarged in bronze.

◉ How do you think Moore felt about being a father?

◉ How has Moore shown the closeness between the two parents?

◉ Which parts of the parents has Moore simplified or exaggerated? What effect does this create?

Family Group
Henry Moore
1948-9 (152cm high)

SCULPTING THE FAMILY

A clay family

Sculpt your own idea of what a family is.

⊙ Shape each person from modelling clay.

⊙ Decide how the people feel about one another and show these feelings in their poses. They might hug one another or stand apart. They might lean towards or away from one another.

Arty tips

✿ Keep hands and faces simple. Tilt, twist or bend parts of the figures to suggest movement and expression.

✿ Exaggerate the size of the feet of standing people so they stay upright.

Alice and Isobel, aged 9, and Rae and Anna, aged 8

Ayesha, aged 7

Louis, Christopher and Alex, aged 9, and Charlie and Farhan, aged 8

Picture hunt

✿ Compare some other family sculptures, such as **The Man-Child** by Frank Dobson, **Mother and Child** by Barbara Hepworth and **Woman with Baby Carriage** by Pablo Picasso.

✿ Look at sculpted figures by Julio Gonzáles, Juan Miró and Alberto Giacometti to discover some other sculptural techniques.

A wire family

Use thin aluminium wire or plastic-coated garden wire to make a dancing family model.

◉ Bend and twist long pieces of wire to shape the figures' heads and bodies.

◉ Wrap around more wire for the arms, legs and hair.

Jazmin and Tessa, aged 8

Alex, aged 9

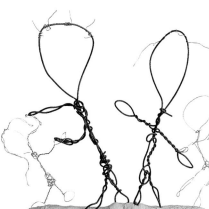

Alice, aged 9

◉ Join some of the people together by the hands.

◉ Stand your sculptures up on a base of modelling clay.

◉ Adjust their poses, to create a feeling of action and liveliness.

Funny families

Create a funny family using clean, empty plastic pots and lids, cardboard rolls and boxes, egg cartons, buttons and other junk.

◉ Use coloured pipe cleaners for hair, arms and legs. Add peel-off stickers for some of the features, as well as for decoration.

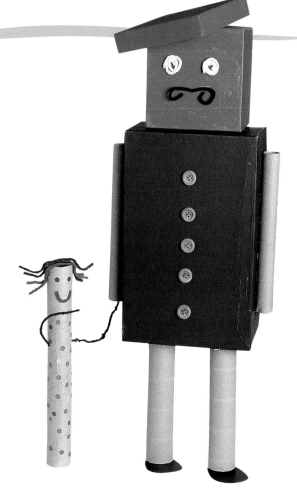

Rubia, Isobel and Sophie, aged 9, and Hannah, aged 8

Christopher and Louis, aged 9, and Declan, Adrian and Charlie, aged 8

FAMILY FEELINGS

The Bellelli Family Edgar Degas
1858-67 (200 x 250cm)

The arrangement of the figures in family portraits can say a lot about their feelings. Here, Degas shows the misery in the family of his aunt, Laure Bellelli. Laure's father, whose portrait hangs on the wall by her head, had recently died. Laure and her two daughters, Giovanna and Giulia, are dressed in black clothes for mourning.

⊙ What clues in the room suggest that the family were quite well off?

A family split

Laure and her husband, Gennaro, were not happy together. Degas used lines and shapes to emphasise the split in the family.

Notice how the sides of the mirror and fireplace, and the table leg, create a dividing line between Gennaro and his family. The armchair also encloses Gennaro, cutting him off from the rest of the room.

Poses and glances

Degas gives more clues about relationships in the family through everyone's posture and expression. He varies the angle of each person's face and eyes to help get the message across.

⊙ How would you describe Laure's pose and expression?

⊙ Where is each person looking? What effect do their gazes have on the image of the family as a whole?

⊙ How does Degas suggest that Giulia (sitting on the chair) might be torn between her two parents?

Cool colours

Artists can use colour to conjure up moods. Here, Degas has used a variety of cold blues and greys to suggest gloom and sadness.

The fire and the candle are deliberately unlit, so there is no warmth in the room. Even the light from the window, reflected in the mirror, feels chilly.

IN THE MOOD

Expressions

Practise drawing faces with all sorts of expressions. Use these examples to help you. Notice how the shape and position of the eyes, nose and mouth change. The closeness or space between the features also helps to create some very different expressions.

happy	sad	angry	frightened	thoughtful

What a feeling!

Draw a family portrait, giving each person an expression and pose that suits his or her personality and feelings.

Jamie, aged 8

Arron, aged 8

Arty tip

✫ Before you draw, think about how you feel when you are sad, angry or frightened and make a suitable face in the mirror. Remember your face and your feelings when you start drawing.

Family life

Draw or paint a picture of an aspect of family life. You might choose an everyday scene. Or you could show the family dressed up for a celebration or going to the cinema or playing in a park.

◉ Add extra details, such as your pets or favourite things that you own, do or wear.

Evie, aged 6

Mary Beth, aged 8

Duncan, aged 9

Flora, aged 8

◉ Try to use colours that express the mood of the occasion – bright colours tend to look happy and lively, while dull colours feel serious or sad.

Picture hunt

✧ Look at pictures that show family life, such as **Pianist and Chequers Players** by Henri Matisse, **Hide and Seek** by James-Jacques-Joseph Tissot, **Portrait of a Family Making Music** by Peter de Hooch and **Sunday Afternnoon** by Fernando Botero.

21

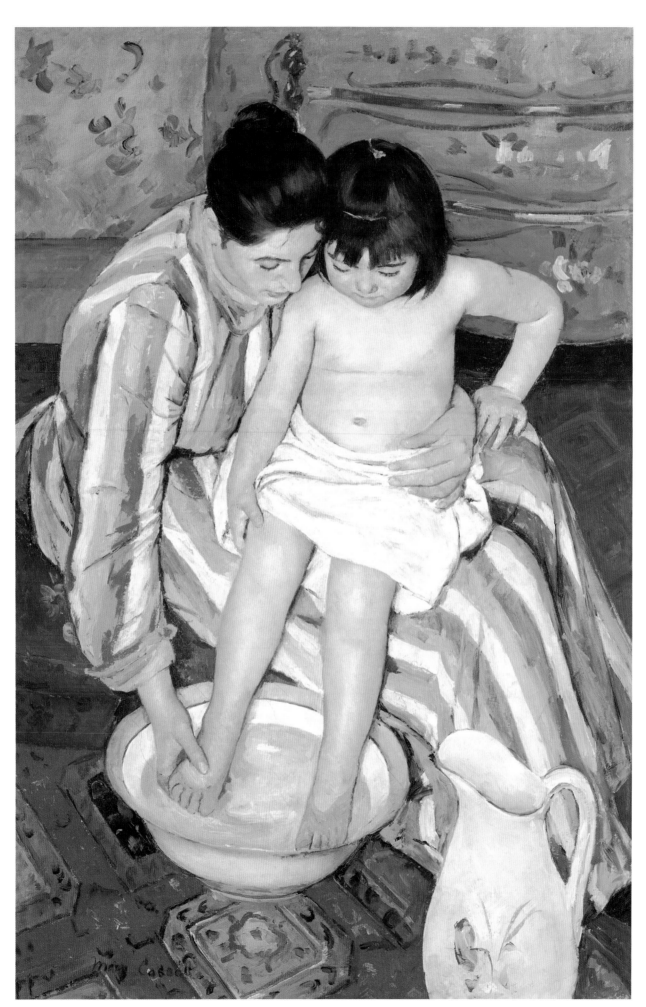

Sometimes, as in these two paintings, artists concentrate on the relationship between just one parent and child.

◉ What are the first differences you notice between the two parent-child relationships pictured here?

Mother and daughter

Cassatt often painted tender, everyday scenes of mothers and children. Her picture on the left was painted at a time when few homes had running water. To make the scene look unposed, Cassatt painted it as if watching from above. Neither figure appears to have noticed the painter, as they both look down at the child's foot in the basin.

◉ How does Cassett show affection between the mother and child?

Father and son

By contrast, Sir Walter Ralegh and his son (*right*) stare boldly out at us. This full-length portrait is a public display of power and ambition. Ralegh was a famous English soldier, explorer and poet, who lived at the time of Queen Elizabeth I. He is said to have introduced tobacco and potatoes to Britain.

Ralegh's stiff pose, with hand on hip, was used by Elizabethan artists to suggest a tough, confident man of action.

◉ What clue shows Ralegh was a soldier?
◉ How would you describe Ralegh's looks and character?
◉ Why do you think Ralegh's son copies his father's pose?

The Bath
Mary Cassatt
1891-92 (100.3 x 66cm)

Sir Walter Ralegh
unknown
1602 (199.4 x 127.3cm)

ME AND YOU

Make the connection

Think how you might show a connection between a parent and child in a picture. It could be a warm hug, a game of football, a shopping trip or even a telling off.

◉ Make pencil sketches of your ideas. Think about how near or far apart you will place the two people and whether or not they will be looking at one another.

◉ Paint a picture of one of your ideas.

Flora, aged 8

Holly, aged 10

Tallissa, aged 9

Jodi, aged 5

Elly, aged 8

Picture hunt

✧ Compare other parent and child paintings, such as **The Cradle** by Berthe Morisot, **The Sick Child** by Edvard Munch, **Augustine Roulin with Marcelle** by Vincent Van Gogh, **Portrait of Alexander J. Cassatt and his Son, Robert Kelso Cassatt** by Mary Cassatt, **Vicomtesse Vilain XIII and her Daughter** by Jacques-Louis David, and any pictures of the Madonna and Child.

Dress to impress

Sir Walter Ralegh and his son dressed in their best outfits for their portraits.

◉ Imagine an artist is going to paint a portrait of you with one of your parents. Design outfits for you both to wear. They can be as wacky as you like!

Kate, aged 9

William, aged 10

Beth, aged 7

Remi, aged 10

Ewen, aged 10

Catherine, aged 5

Sam, aged 11

Alex, aged 7

Arty tips

✰ Use repeating colours for both people if you want to emphasise the links between them. Use contrasting colours and shapes to stress differences.

✰ You could create a collage by adding decoration such as fabric, ribbon, buttons, glitter or beads.

25

THE FAMILY ALBUM

A century ago, few people owned cameras. Having a family photo taken was a big event. People dressed in their smartest clothes and went to a photographer's studio.

Family in focus

Family photos were carefully composed to make everyone look their best. They often included props, such as painted back-cloths, velvet drapes and fancy chairs.

◉ Compare these two family photographs:

● How did the photographers make sure that everyone in the family could be clearly seen?
● Who is the focus of each photo? How can you tell?
● How did the photographers link the family members?

Painterly poses

Many photographs were inspired by painted portraits.
◉ What similarities are there between the photograph on the right and the family portrait shown on page 4?

Family photographs taken at portrait photographers' studios

George, Blanche, Celia, Albert and Percy
David Hockney
1983
(111 x 118cm)

A photomontage

This picture is made from lots of colour photographs. Hockney took a variety of close-up shots of this family in their sitting room with their cats. He overlapped the photos and stuck them together to make a collage, called a photomontage.

From start to finish

Hockney's arrangement of the photos shows the family members at several different moments in time. Notice how their heads, bodies and hands shift and their expressions change from one photo to the next. Look at the cats as well.

◉ How many photographs are there of each person's head?

◉ How has Hockney included himself and the rest of the room in the picture?

◉ What differences are there between this family picture and the old ones taken in photographic studios?

FAMILY SNAPSHOTS

Strike a pose!

Take your own specially posed family photographs. Think about these things before you start:

- Will you take the photos inside or outside your house or elsewhere?
- How will people pose?
- Will you take photos close up (just faces) or from further away?
- Will people dress up smartly?
- Will you ask people to look at the camera or at one another?
- Will they be smiling or serious?
- Will you include cousins, uncles, aunts, grandparents or any pets?

Andrew, aged 5

Christopher, aged 9

Rachel, aged 9

Jamie, aged 8

Frances, aged 11

Emile, aged 5

Arty tips

✧ If you want to capture people's characters in the photo, tell them to act naturally and don't warn them when you're about to take the picture. Take several 'surprise' shots.

✧ If you want to be in your own photos, find out how to use the self-timer. Or ask a friend to take the shot once you've fixed the pose.

People puzzle

Make your own family photomontage.

◉ Blow up a family photo to A4 using a photocopier.

◉ Make several copies of it.

◉ Cut each copy into 4cm squares.

◉ Arrange the squares on some card or on a background, perhaps cut from a magazine. Overlap the squares or glue them side by side.

◉ Exaggerate parts of the photo by using the same mini-image several times.

Indi, aged 11

Morphing

If your school or family has a digital camera, experiment with the photo-editing software to create morphing effects like these.

◉ Download some digital images onto your computer.

◉ Open an image with your photo-editing software.

◉ Click on the 'effects' tab on the toolbar or see what choices drop down from the 'edit' bar.

◉ Select and click on an effect. Your photograph will instantly transform itself!

Todd, aged 8

original photo

oil painting

sketch

splash

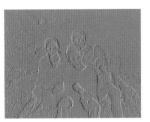
melting

wrinkle

mosaic

emboss

fish eye

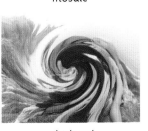
whirlpool

ribbon

spiral

29

ARTISTS AND ANSWERS

FAMILIES FOREVER (pages 4/5)

About WILLIAM HOGARTH

Hogarth (1697-1764) was an English artist who trained as an engraver. He then set up as a portrait painter, but also painted comical pictures that told stories with a moral. He ran his own painting academy for 20 years and created the first permanent public gallery of English art. This was the main forerunner of London's famous Royal Academy.

About JACOB LAWRENCE

Lawrence (1917–2000) was an African-American artist, known for his pictures about the life and culture of black people in America. He painted portraits of black heroes and heroines, everyday scenes in the neighbourhood of Harlem, New York, and series of pictures showing both the achievements and the struggles of black people.

FAMILY FORTUNES (pages 6/7)

Answers for page 7

• The father indicates that his son will be his heir by pointing to him with his forefinger. The son also stands higher than his sisters and next to his father.
• The boy seems proud and haughty.
• The eldest daughter is the one next to the son. She has one foot on the platform and stands apart from the other two girls in a more active pose.

About ANTHONY VAN DYCK

Van Dyck (1599-1641) was born in Antwerp in Flanders (now Belgium). He trained as a painter from the age of ten. In his teens, he became an assistant to Rubens, the most famous Flemish artist of the time. His early pictures, of saints and Bible stories, were painted for churches. Later he travelled to England and Italy, where he worked on elegant, imposing portraits of kings, courtiers and other important people. In London he became court painter to Charles I, who paid him a large salary and gave him a knighthood.

A FAMILY TREE (pages 10/11)

Answers for page 11

• Frida used a ribbon to link the family. Red suggests blood ties.
• Frida has added herself as a curled-up foetus attached to her mother in the painting. In the photograph, Frida's father leans towards her mother.
• The strongest person is perhaps the father, who, together with Frida, is at the centre of the picture and seems to shelter her. Frida was deeply fond of her father.

About FRIDA KAHLO

Kahlo (1907-1954) was a Mexican artist. She started painting at the age of 19, encouraged by Diego Rivera, the famous Mexican mural painter, whom she married. Kahlo mainly painted people she knew, or self-portraits. In some self-portraits she wore bright Mexican clothes and included her favourite pet monkeys or birds. In others she showed images of her thoughts and feelings.

MODEL FAMILIES (pages 14/15)

Answers for pages 14 and 15

• Marisol's family is tense. None of the people touch one another and the father stands back. In Moore's family, the figures are close and intertwined.
• The upright stiffness and squareness of the figures makes them look serious and formal.
• The mother has a carved head, hands and legs. The father's face and body are painted.
• The girl has three legs. The babies' feet are adult-sized.
• The pram, the man's trouser legs and shoes are ready-made. The head, hats, hands and legs of the women and children are carved. The man's head and body and the woman's body are painted on wood.

• Moore was thrilled to be a father.
• Moore showed closeness by linking the parents' arms around their child.
• Moore's parents have small heads and almost no features. The curve of their
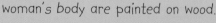
backs is exaggerated and their legs are elongated to create a feeling of security and protectiveness.

About MARISOL (ESCOBAR)

Marisol (b.1930) was born in Paris to Venezuelan parents. When she was 20, she moved to New York, where she still lives. Her sculptures are often inspired by photographs of ordinary people, especially families. These combine drawing and painting with carving and ready-made objects. She has also made casts of faces and limbs, arranged into artworks. Sometimes, she includes images of herself in her work.

About HENRY MOORE

Moore (1898-1976) was an English artist. He trained as a teacher before becoming a sculptor. The main themes in his work were reclining women and mother-and-child. Their shapes were often greatly simplified, sometimes with holes pierced through them. They were mostly carved in stone or wood. During World War II, Moore was a war artist and drew people in bomb shelters. As his fame and demand for his work grew, he started making large works for public places, which were usually cast in bronze.

FAMILY FEELINGS (pages 18/19)

Answers for page 19

• The furniture and carpet, fancy clock, decorated plates, gilt mirror and gold candlesticks suggest wealth.
• Laure's pose is stiff and tense. Her expression is thoughtful and dreamy.
• No-one in the picture looks at anyone else. This gives a feeling of tension and distance.
• Giulia's head turns towards her father and her body and foot are twisted towards her mother.

About EDGAR DEGAS

Degas (1834-1917) was a French painter who exhibited with the Impressionists – artists who were interested in painting scenes of modern life. Many Impressionists painted outdoors, trying to capture the effects of sunlight on a scene. Degas was more interested in movement and the effects of artifical lights at theatres and the circus. He captured dancers rehearsing as well as performing. He also painted scenes of horse races, women bathing and portraits. In old age, when bad eyesight made drawing difficult, he modelled dancers and horses in clay or wax.

TWO OF A KIND (pages 22/23)

Answers for page 23

• The Cassatt picture shows a warm, close relationship between parent and child. The Ralegh portrait shows a stiff, more distant relationship.
• Cassatt shows affection by the closeness of the two figures. Their heads touch and the mother leans towards the child and holds her securely on her lap.
• Ralegh wears a sword to show he is a soldier.
• Ralegh seems good-looking, dignified and confident.
• Ralegh wanted his son to follow in his footsteps as an important soldier, so the son copies his pose.

About MARY CASSATT

Cassatt (1844-1926) was an American painter. She studied art in Pennsylvania and then in Paris, where she lived for the rest of her life. Her work was noticed by Edgar Degas, who invited her to exhibit with the Impressionists and later became a good friend. Cassatt mainly painted oil or pastel portraits of her family and friends, at home or at the theatre.

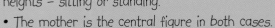

THE FAMILY ALBUM (pages 26/27)

Answers for pages 26 and 27

• Everyone is visible because they are at different heights – sitting or standing.
• The mother is the central figure in both cases.
• People are linked either with their arms or elbows.
• The eldest son and daughter are nearest to the father; the mother is sitting in the middle; they wear their best clothes.
• There are at least three pictures of each family member's head.
• Hockney and the room are reflected in the mirror.

• The studio photos show still, solemn and stiff families. Hockney's picture shows a more relaxed family in their own surroundings and gives a sense of action and lively conversation. It also includes pets.

About DAVID HOCKNEY

Hockney (b.1937) is an English artist who first became known as a painter. He is particularly famous for his portraits and interiors, which use strong, flat colours with a focus on light and reflections. He has also done stage designs for ballets and operas, made films, experimented with photomontages, fax art and computer prints, and created many book illustrations.

GLOSSARY

coat of arms A decorative emblem that is the symbol of a particular family.

collage A picture made by sticking bits of paper, fabric, or other objects, on to a background.

family tree A chart that shows how the generations of a family are related.

generation A family level. You are a generation below your parents, your children will be the next generation, and so on.

heir The person who will take on, or inherit, the property of a dead person.

morphing To distort an image, usually digitally.

photomontage A collage made up of photographs.

portrait An image of a particular person or group of people.

pose A physical position, or the action of getting into a position deliberately eg posing for a portrait.

studio An artist's or photographer's workplace.